AF306737

Tucholsky Wagner Zola Scott Sydow Freud Schlegel
Turgenev Fonatne Wallace
Twain Walther von der Vogelweide Fouqué Friedrich II. von Preußen
Weber Freiligrath Frey
Fechner Fichte Weiße Rose von Fallersleben Kant Ernst Frommel
Richthofen
Engels Fielding Hölderlin
Fehrs Faber Flaubert Eichendorff Tacitus Dumas
Eliasberg Ebner Eschenbach
Maximilian I. von Habsburg Fock Zweig
Feuerbach Eliot Vergil
Ewald London
Goethe Elisabeth von Österreich
Mendelssohn Balzac Shakespeare Dostojewski Ganghofer
Lichtenberg Rathenau Doyle Gjellerup
Trackl Stevenson Hambruch
Mommsen Tolstoi Lenz Droste-Hülshoff
Thoma Hanrieder
Dach Verne Hägele Hauff Humboldt
von Arnim
Reuter Rousseau Hagen Hauptmann Gautier
Karrillon Garschin
Defoe Baudelaire
Damaschke Hebbel
Descartes Hegel Kussmaul Herder
Wolfram von Eschenbach Schopenhauer Rilke George
Bronner Darwin Dickens
Melville Grimm Jerome Bebel Proust
Campe Horváth Aristoteles Voltaire Federer Herodot
Bismarck Vigny Barlach Heine
Gengenbach
Storm Casanova Tersteegen Grillparzer Georgy
Chamberlain Lessing Gilm
Langbein Gryphius
Brentano Lafontaine
Strachwitz Claudius Schiller Kralik Iffland Sokrates
Katharina II. von Rußland Bellamy Schilling
Gerstäcker Raabe Gibbon Tschechow
Löns Hesse Hoffmann Gogol Wilde Vulpius
Luther Heym Hofmannsthal Gleim
Roth Klee Hölty Morgenstern Goedicke
Luxemburg Heyse Klopstock Kleist
Machiavelli La Roche Puschkin Homer Mörike Musil
Horaz
Navarra Aurel Musset Kierkegaard Kraft Kraus
Lamprecht Kind Moltke
Nestroy Marie de France Kirchhoff Hugo
Laotse Ipsen Liebknecht
Nietzsche Nansen Ringelnatz
Marx Lassalle Gorki Klett
von Ossietzky Leibniz
May vom Stein Lawrence Irving
Petalozzi Knigge
Platon Michelangelo Kafka
Pückler
Sachs Poe Kock
Liebermann Korolenko
de Sade Praetorius Mistral Zetkin

The publishing house tredition has created the series **TREDITION CLASSICS**. It contains classical literature works from over two thousand years. Most of these titles have been out of print and off the bookstore shelves for decades.

The book series is intended to preserve the cultural legacy and to promote the timeless works of classical literature. As a reader of a **TREDITION CLASSICS** book, the reader supports the mission to save many of the amazing works of world literature from oblivion.

The symbol of **TREDITION CLASSICS** is Johannes Gutenberg (1400 – 1468), the inventor of movable type printing.

With the series, tredition intends to make thousands of international literature classics available in printed format again – worldwide.

All books are available at book retailers worldwide in paperback and in hardcover. For more information please visit: www.tredition.com

tredition was established in 2006 by Sandra Latusseck and Soenke Schulz. Based in Hamburg, Germany, tredition offers publishing solutions to authors and publishing houses, combined with worldwide distribution of printed and digital book content. tredition is uniquely positioned to enable authors and publishing houses to create books on their own terms and without conventional manufacturing risks.

For more information please visit: www.tredition.com

Confiscation; an outline

William Greenwood

Imprint

This book is part of the TREDITION CLASSICS series.

Author: William Greenwood
Cover design: toepferschumann, Berlin (Germany)

Publisher: tredition GmbH, Hamburg (Germany)
ISBN: 978-3-8491-6641-0

www.tredition.com
www.tredition.de

Copyright:
The content of this book is sourced from the public domain.

The intention of the TREDITION CLASSICS series is to make world literature in the public domain available in printed format. Literary enthusiasts and organizations worldwide have scanned and digitally edited the original texts. tredition has subsequently formatted and redesigned the content into a modern reading layout. Therefore, we cannot guarantee the exact reproduction of the original format of a particular historic edition. Please also note that no modifications have been made to the spelling, therefore it may differ from the orthography used today.

WILLIAM GREENWOOD

Those Palaces on the Nob Hills of these United States; are the toadstools of the decay that is going on in this Republic today. -

PREFACE.

The Emancipation Proclamation has only 718 words.

Lincoln's address at Gettysburg has only 266 Words.

The works of Thomas Paine were not only one of the important factors that brought success to the struggle for Independence, but they were also largely instrumental in the Declaration itself being made. And those works, what were they? - mere pamphlets.

Shakespeare, whose writings are said to be an education in themselves, can be had in a volume not twice the size of "Progress and Poverty."

Why, then, cannot a scheme of political economy, even when it is a radical departure from our present system, be sufficiently outlined for working purposes in a volume of this size, and also written so that it shall be intelligible to those to whom all such works should in a Republic be addressed; namely, the voter, who alone has the power to bring about the desired change?

The late Professor Tyndall was both an original investigator of natural phenomena and a teacher who could make his discoveries plain to the ordinary mind as he could to the scientist working in the same field as himself.

Discovering a truth in Nature or in political economies is work only half done if the discoverer wishes to make it known to those in whose interest he claims to be working.

Labor, iron labor, makes the scholar, says Emerson.

Labor, iron labor, gave Tyndall the faculty that, made him intelligible and interesting to the young, and the right to preside at a meeting of Humboldts.

But there is pride of intellect as well as pride of riches, and none shows this pride as do the writers on political economy who have made it the "dismal science," instead of having made it the A, B, C of our mental furniture, as it should be with the people of a republic.

Making a good use of our means in our home and business affairs is good economics.

Making a poor use of them is bad economics.

That is all there is to this word, whether it is our private affairs or those of the nation that are being considered.

If we live up to our laws, and yet want and privation exist while there is more than sufficient for all, then the fault must, be in those laws.

Making a scapegoat of the foreigner for those conditions because he will not buy our wheat, or use a metal that we have an overplus of, places us side by side with the witch-burner of old. We are just as ignorant in one way, as he was in another.

At his door who has been writing on this subject does the blame of this universal ignorance of it belong. He takes up this plain, simple subject, and becomes an intellectual aristocrat and a snob of exclusiveness from that time on, and, like the aristocrat of wealth, will have nothing further to do with the common people, cutting off all former connections by turning out a mass of intellectual mud that, only leisure and education can penetrate. And dear to him is the dignity of bulk, the dignity of paunch, using, as he does, twenty words where three would do better work. The living and the dead if his species are alike in this hunt for the "Absolutely Pure" to puff out their little dough.

Dissecting "Co-operation," the writer of Progress and Poverty must drag the poor remains through over 800 words - almost enough to bury the single tax theory itself. Co-operation means getting rid of the middleman. With organized labor it, means keeping out all whose admittance would cause a surplus of labor among those who have organized to prevent that as well as injustice by the employer. But what has become of that middleman and black-balled laborer? One is ruined and the other is a helpless chip that is drifting into - some State prison for forty years.

Co-operation is the savior of some, but the ruination of others, and her plea of justifiable homicide cannot be accepted while this earth has more than enough for her own.

Not a God-like wisdom, nor the assumption of it, is needed to either conceive a remedy for our present troubles, or to formulate laws for its application. Plain sense we most all have, let us use it, then, and we will have no further use for either the bookworm or the logic chopper.

Confiscation.

I.

Running a republic under the economic laws of a monarchy must of necessity result in producing the same conditions - great wealth for some and great poverty for the rest. This may be a government by the people, but it certainly is no longer a government for the people. Heretofore individual greed has had full swing in the United States, and naturally enough the ablest returned in possession of everything worth grabbing. And naturally enough, too, if a republic means a country owned by all its people, it cannot be a republic if it is owned by only a few. All the power of a country is bound to be in the hands of those who own it. If its wealth is in the hands of a few, its power is there with it. In the hands of a few it must be, if it would be a kingdom or empire. In the hands of all it must be, if it would be a republic. To insist on having the personal liberty that goes with a republic, and at the same time not to set a limit to the resources an individual can own, is a contradiction. A republic has economic laws that are essential to her existence. Any others mean her destruction. And it is utterly out of the question for any political party to improve the conditions of the people, while they use the present economic laws as the basis of their proposed legislation.

You must begin at the foundation. Individual greed should be made to respect the right of others to exist, and made to conform itself to laws that are as necessary to the life of a republic as is the ballot itself. The ballot, in fact, has lost its power. It is the key to a house we have lost possession of, and if we would regain possession and make the ballot something more than a mere symbol of a thing that is dead, we have no choice but to resort to the one process by which the resources of the country can be returned to its people, and the blight of poverty and pauperism that is settling down on the country and is becoming permanent can be removed - namely, confiscation.

Man, in the beginning, seeing annihilation staring him in the face, combined and gave us the Government of the Tribe; out of that developed the Despotic form; out of that developed the Constitutional Monarchy, out of which developed the Republic, the highest type of them all; and this work of development must ever go on, if we would not lapse into former conditions.

The founders of the republic could not have expected their work to so soon come to the Chinese halt that has overtaken it, until we now find ourselves floating on an ebbing sea back to the shores we thought we had forever left behind.

The founders of the republic met the needs of their hour, and expelled the foreigner. We have failed to meet the need of our hour in not discarding the economic laws that were of that foreigner's bringing; the economic laws of the monarchist and despotic forms of government, that is making this republic a republic only in name: the economic laws of the monarchist and despotic forms of government that has built up an aristocracy of wealth here as they have there, that must of necessity depend here for its existence as it does there, on the enslavement of the people. Do not let a mere word further deceive you. The word republic means a free people - we are slaves. For great revenue, be it of king or millionaire, has the same magician's wand - the overladen back of the enslaved toiler.

In the face of our boasted intelligence what an appalling sight does this country offer to the All-seeing Eye. An abundance of everything and people starving by the thousands. When our lawmakers in Washington learned that the death penalty was to be inflicted on those who were convicted of treason for trying to overthrow the established government in Hawaii, they said it must not be done, and busied themselves to save those people's lives. And during all their agitation to save these men who were to suffer a punishment that is meted out to such by all governments, thousands of their own people were perishing for the want of something to eat - not inhuman or hard-hearted, but simply do not see how they can prevent it. There is no law by which they can stop starvation. The legislator in a monarchy knows that poverty is inseparable from that form of government and are reconciled to it.

Our legislators are reconciled to the same conditions. They do not see the incongruity of conforming the legislation of a republic to the economic laws of a monarchy. They do not know what a government by the people and for the people means. If they did, they would know that there was something wrong when one man has

$50,000,00 while another has not enough to get his shoes cobbled: and another has 50,000 acres of land, while others must be buried four in a grave.

And none of the political parties shows a way of escape out of this miserable state of affairs, as a brief review of their positions will show.

We once had the Free States and the Slave States, and these two terms were designative of two sections into which the country was then divided on the question of slavery. To-day we have "Free Coinage of Silver," "Protection," and "Free Trade." These three terms, Free Coinage of Silver, Protection, and Free Trade, are as truly designative of three different sections into which the country is divided to-day on economic or industrial questions as were the terms Free States and Slave States designative of two sections in the past. Thus the preponderating interest in one section is the mining of silver, and this interest is represented by the Populist Party, who demands the coinage of more Silver. The preponderating interest of the second section, or East, is manufactures, and is represented by the Republican Party, who demands protection. The preponderating interest of the third section, or South, is agriculture, and is repre-sented by the Democratic Party, who demands free trade. This is substantially correct, although the Populists seem to be as strong in the agricultural South as in the silver-producing West. The Populist Party, indeed, originated among, the agriculturists of the South, and was the outgrowth of discontent among the farmers; and in saying that Populism has its stronghold in the West, or silver-producing section, we simply mean that the farmers' organization has been captured by the silver interest. They seem to think that their own prosperity is linked with that of the silver producers, and that the free coinage of silver means the salvation of both. With this political manoeuvering, however, we have nothing to do. There are three political parties in the field, each with the preponderating interest of some section in charge, which it is bound to see through regardless of the interests of the other two. The industrial rivalry that is going on throughout the whole world has entered these United States, and each of the three different sections are struggling to obtain legisla-tion favorable to itself, with the same indifference to the interests of the others that is shown by France to England or by England to the

United States. Even the naked savage has found that it is a good thing to have something to sell, and our agriculturists are brought into competition with territory the New World over where a plow or harvester was unknown ten years ago; instead of having a monopoly in the European markets, as was the case a few years ago, where they could dispose of their surplus, they are now compelled to feed it to their hogs, which, as a source of profit, ranks even now with the thing they are fed on.

But we are not depending on foreign markets for enough to eat and wear. Those things are here, not there. We may have lost the foreigner as a customer, but what prevents us from eating that which he refuses to buy. We look back a hundred or more years, and cry out in horror at the inhumanity of those then in power, in allowing human beings to be burned alive and living creatures to be torn to pieces on the rack. Those who will look back to these times will be no less astounded at the inhumanity and imbecility of those now in power in allowing starvation while food is actually rotting for the want of consumers. The question, then, is, can we not formulate a policy that will work harmoniously throughout the whole country for the benefit of all sections and every individual? Can we not find some way out of the swamp into which the masterful greed of a few and the dense stupidity of their legislative tools have mired us?

If we cannot, then let us submit, with the best grace possible to our masters who know how to lay on the lash when their dividends are at stake.

The resources of the United States have hardly been touched upon; but in less than a hundred years individual greed has done its work, and the people are bankrupt. They have been legislated out of everything, and the one function of our government, as at present conducted, is to see that this legislation is enforced. Yes, it is beyond the reach of contradiction that this government, that was founded in the interests of All, has degenerated into a merciless taskmaster, ever ready to beat into submission the slaves of the country, when their few owners give the word.

But this treatment should be expected. It goes with ownership. Give me the ownership of men, and all else goes with the title - how

I shall clothe, feed, and lodge them, and how I shall keep them on the grind. Of course, the wise ones will say, Was it not our own chosen representatives who made all those laws that gave our resources and the people themselves over to the favored few, and must not we, the principals, grin and bear it, and live up to whatever contracts those representatives, our agents, made in our name?

It is not, however, how we were despoiled, but how we are to recover the plunder, that is interesting us just now. Is there a way out of the night of despair? is the question that should be met, and, if possible, answered. Finding a way out of a difficulty is one thing, however, and having the courage to take it is another. Modern surgery has discovered much, but without the courage to use the knife mankind would not have been the gainer. The prayer meeting has its uses, but those who expect to obtain political or industrial deliverance in that quarter can set out their rain-gauges and go there; but those who know the nature of the fellow who has been grabbing all in sight will make him let go in the old-time way by using a force superior to his own - a force that he will feel when it comes down, supposing the power to feel is left in him.

We have no hatred of the rich - nor love of the poor, for that matter. They are both fishers for gain, and one gets it, and the other don't; but his basket is just as large. But we are a lover of justice, and if one is too much for the other would handicap him, and thereby make the struggle for existence more even for both. The weakling, will always be a weakling, whatever laws are passed for his benefit, and the drudgery of the world will ever be his portion; from it he can never escape, but he is entitled to his life, and if the able denies him, what is necessary to it, then Justice must step in and take his part.

Volumes could be padded in showing how this can be done, but we can demonstrate in this brief work how poverty can be obliterated as a feature of our national life, and if it does not make justice more even-handed for all, and the people of this country as prosperous as any on earth, then the fault must be in the plan itself, and not in the resources which we possess, for of those we have enough to empty every poorhouse in the land, and eighty-five per cent. of the jails and penitentiaries.

Let our wrongs be righted without physical force, by all means. History, however, has no encouragement for such a hope. The contentions with those on top have ever been of the blood-red order. Power once obtained has never been surrendered only through conquest. The ballot should do much, and had it been in use in the past history might have had less of blood in it, as it should have less of it in the future. But the ballot for a long number of years has, like a great many stomachs of late, been working on wind - the wind of the Protectionist, the wind of the Free Trader, and the wind of the latest cure-all, the fellow who is hunting a market for his silver.

If something substantial to work on is not soon given to this man with the ballot, he will drop it - and then let the blame of it rest with the fools and rascals who have been deluding him so long.

The average man makes a better soldier than he does a voter. He can get the range of an object easier than he can comprehend an economic truth - this one, for instance: If the capitalists have obtained possession of the money issued in the past, what is to prevent them from getting possession of all that will be issued in the future? His answer will be to issue more. He has been told so by his political mentor. When the man with the ballot loses confidence in this mentor, he will start a game of his own, and then the jig will be up with that idiot. We use the word idiot advisedly here. When a tax was assessed against the incomes of the rich, this driveler would score a point gained in favor of the people. This claim of itself shows the institution to which he should be consigned.

Victoria, Empress and Queen, rules a country where, pauperism is steadily on the increase, and the potter's field received the bodies of eighty of her subjects that were frozen to death in London in four days of January last. Yet the rich have been paying an income tax in that country for generations past.

When the rich merchant, or rich anything else, insures what he is dealing in, he adds the cost of his policy to the thing he sells. The income tax is but another premium, and he tags that on where he pinned the other. The laborer has always paid the expenses of the rich, and always will. The laborer can never dictate terms to the rich. The labor leaders even have come to recognize the hopelessness of the unequal contest. The power of the rich to do as they like can never be destroyed while they are allowed to retain the riches that gives them this power. A readjustment and a limit set to the amount an individual can own is the only remedy. And the sooner that unassailable truth is recognized and acted upon, the sooner will you get rid of the lobbiest and the pauper.

II.

We need more money per capita: say some more would-be leaders, who have found the only way out of the land of bondage. Increase the currency to $50 per capita, and business and prosperity will once more fill the land. Money has become scarcer, they continue, and therefore dearer. Those who contracted monetary obligations last week find that they are now paying more for the use of that money than it was worth when the debt was made.

This is a hardship on the borrower, and can be prevented by increasing the amount of money in circulation.

This is the very essence of what is claimed by those who are for increasing the volume of money in circulation. Money has changed in value, and those who are mortgaged, or otherwise under interest-paying obligations, have found that money is scarcer, in this instance through contraction of the currency, and therefore harder to get.

There should certainly be enough money issued for the smooth carrying on of the country's business, and when they determine the amount necessary, it should be put in circulation at once. But stopping money from fluctuating value is another thing.

The man who buys a barrel of flour one day for $4.00 may find that it is worth only $3.50 the day after. The man who borrows money at 7 per cent. one day may find it worth only 6 1/2 the day after.

To prevent these fluctuations in the value of either money or commodities is a legislative feat beyond the power of mortal man. And when we see our Legislator trying to regulate the value of anything that one man has to sell to another, are no longer surprised at his trying to regulate the weather by exploding powder in the air. Our Mark Twains and Bill Nyes are flat indeed, when compared to that straight-faced clown, the American legislator, who would give an unchangable value to either the shoes we wear or the money we use.

This whole question of currency has as little to do with the prevailing misery as the missing button off your vest would have to do with your being frozen to death. England not only has enough money to carry on her own business, but also has $15,000,000,000 to lend to outsiders. It is not the wealth of a country, but how it is distributed that tells the story.

-

The single taxers of whom Henry George is the great apostle, are also claiming the floor, but a patient hearing finds the distressed turning away for relief that the single taxer can not give. They are cultivating a century plant, and while we are waiting for it to bloom three generations of human beings will have met their millionaire masters and taken their place in the line that leads to the soup house and the pauper's grave.

The masterly logic of these reformers is the work of serene-tempered and well-fed men, whose cosy library with windows facing to the south, and the open fire-place with its soothing and cheerful glow, is conducive to the developing of a red-tape reform that must be an inspiring subject for discussion at an afternoon tea. Because they are well fed is the reason why they can play a waiting game, but the despairing and maddened people, for whose benefit this single tax contract, with its long deferred payment, is being drawn up, will have as little use for it as they will have for the plate-glass window when their bread riots begin.

The land owner alone is the one these one-horse-chaise reformers would start their Dobbin after. The large landowner should be cut down in his holdings, and their plan is just the one to fix him and make him let go. They will tax him in such a way that he cannot pay, and then they have got him, they tell us, as they leisurely jog along over their pleasant highway.

Now, why this dilly-dallying with the large land-owner, or any one else, that has something that he should surrender for the general good?

When the owning of 50,000 acres of land by one man is wrong, then it is wrong to let him own it, and if there was one drop of the John Brown blood in this crew of house-gown and plush-slipper reformers, they would go into the enemy's camp, and never let up on their open warfare until what belonged to the people was returned to them.

Taxing an enemy to make him give up his plunder!

When hunger and plenty is found side by side what solution can there be but to set a limit to what the overendowed can tag with his name, and to put his forfeited surplus where the underfed can, with reasonable labor, get possession of it.

If the single taxer is given plenty of time, he will accomplish something, undoubtedly, but the whole thing will be over long before poor old Dobbin gets on to the scene.

-

The millionaire land-owner and the millionaire capitalist are as much out of place in a republic as is the man with a title; and the laws which permitted the growth of the first two are the primary cause of the disgraceful conditions that exist in this Republic to-day. When we know that people in actual want are to be found in every section of the United States, we ought to be able to say that it is Nature that has failed us for the time being; but it is not Nature, but the wretched laws of man's own making that are at fault. Had we the economic laws that belong to a republic, instead of those that belong to a despotism, the foreign markets could be entirely closed to us, and all our people would still have enough of all things that are necessary to life. And those able men who have gone into the domain of natural philosophy, to see what they could find to advance and benefit the human race, have found so much, and brought about such a change in the industrial world, that they have completely bewildered our political philosophers, who have been utterly unable to make room for the labor-saving inventions and discoveries of those men, until the confusion and distress resulting from the incompetence of our political philosophers to adjust the laws to meet the changed conditions are beginning to make us look upon the inventors as our enemies, instead of our benefactors.

The work of the world consists principally in raising food and manufacturing the things we wear, and the forwarding of both to the consumer. And the great inventions of the McCormicks, Howes,

Fultons, Stephensons, and rest have made this work so easy that the labor done in two months now is equivalent to the labor done in twelve months a few years ago. That is why they are great inventions. Yet our law-makers are still legislating for conditions that disappeared with the ox-goad, hand loom, lapstone, and sickle, and are continually trying to devise ways and means by which the labor of the country can be kept employed the year round. What doing? When they find out how to make you wear twenty pairs of shoes at a time, they will have found out how to keep the shoe factories running the year round, not before.

The natural philosopher can overcome physical difficulties; the political philosopher cannot overcome economic ones.

We would reside on a certain hill were it not for the climb. A Hallidie lays his cable, and puts us at the top without further trouble. We find Egypt cutting into our cotton market, Argentine into our wheat market, France and Germany have shut their doors against our meats, and England will not approve of silver. Many throughout this country find their very bread falling short through these conditions abroad, and the sufferers call in our political economists to help them to at least keep the necessaries of life within their reach.

Of the various nostrums prescribed by these political quacks, two have been thoroughly tried, but the aggravating results have only cut the eye-teeth of the humbugged; and when they take the field themselves as political economists they will have a preparation of their own that will be bitter enough to the taste of those to whom they will apply it.

III.

What rainbow-chasers these McKinleys, Wilsons, and J. P. Joneses are! Do they not see this country with its limitless resources? Do they not see the surfeited millionaire, and the hungry laborer with his starving dependents? Do they not see that they must break down the one if they would build up the other? Do not these miserable bunglers see that this noble ship of the fathers is foundering because of her uneven load?

See the imbeciles rushing hither and thither in frantic despair! This, one with his wad of wool to stop a leak that does not exist; that one with his tears and kisses falling on the silver charm that hangs about his neck; this other at the masthead high shouting to foreign Shores for help we do not need.

Never did the black flag of a Caesar or a Napoleon III. bear down on a richer-laden prey than this helpless hulk and its jabbering crew.

-

Through Confiscation, and Confiscation alone, can we restore the conditions that are necessary to the life of the Republic.

Confiscation is a forbidding word. We associate it with the sheriff's writ, and with the idea of distress in some form, and with bloody war itself, its greatest field of operation. It is one of the few words in the vocabulary of Might. Without Might there would be no such word, and the weak have ever been the prey of both. But it is a plain word. As plain as are the conditions under which we are now living. There is no mistaking its meaning. And having the same momentous work ahead of us - of gaining our freedom, and throwing off the yoke of our latest master - as that which confronted the founders of the Republic, we cannot go to a nursery rhyme for a word to describe that work.

It is the way in which Might is to restore our lost liberties and resources that is of the gravest concern to all, and not the word used to describe the result of what Might shall do.

Justice is due. But how is it to arrive? By way of the ballot, or over the same bloodstained road in use before the ballot was discovered?

If the plundered and starving have lost faith in the ballot, and sheer want has brutalized them until they see no way but the brute's way of saving themselves, then place the horror of it all at the doors of incompetence and grasping greed where it belongs.

It is a plain word. As plain as are the conditions under which we are now living. As plain as is the wide-spread want and hunger that is in this land to-day, while there is more than enough for all.

And those who have gained possession of our resources are responsible for this hunger, and are enemies just as much as if they were invaders. Whatever progress external foes could make in landing on these shores would be only temporary, and not a blow could they strike, or a step make, without our knowing it. Not so the millionaire. His is the work of the thief in the night and we know nothing till his work is done. And then, because we would resort to the same process of recovery that we would in the case of any common enemy, we hold back, forsooth, because that process is called Confiscation.

Those whom we find to be inimical to the life of the republic will look upon an anarchist as a cooing dove compared to the man who would advocate Confiscation. They have nothing to fear from the anarchist, except a stray bomb now and then, for they know full well that the "plain" people will always stand between them and that wild-eyed dreamer of the impractical.

What those favored people think, however, does not interest us. What is of more concern to us, and to all others who have no doubt but what there is something wrong in the present scheme of things, is that the doctrine of Confiscation should be first understood before it is rejected. If it is found to conflict with law and order; if it is found to obstruct in any way the material welfare necessary to any man, woman, or child in the United States; if if takes from any man, woman, or child in these United States a solitary privilege or right that is essential to their well being; if it makes one more tramp, convict, or outcast of the street; if it fills one more pauper's bed or potter's grave, then our Search is not ended, for it is only another delusion, and of them we have more than enough already.

If, on the other hand, it does away with hunger and rags in a land of plenty. Does away with the cause of ignorance, namely poverty. Does away with the cause of eighty-five per cent. of crime, namely, poverty. Does away with the cause of strikes and rioting, namely, poverty. Destroys the power of one man to bribe one or fifty, and with his thumb at his nose defies the law to reach him. Makes robbery of the people by way of the lobby a thing of the past, and makes unnecessary a third house for the investigation of the other two, a stage we have already reached. Does away with the millionaire and his charity - the beggar and his need of it. Gives the conditions which makes individual and national improvement possible, and securing every such national improvement by making all the people its willing defenders, which they are far from being now in their hunger and wretchedness. Makes employment easy to obtain, with just wages in return for the labor done, putting within the reach of all, those comforts and luxuries, which, in this age of the world with its skill for quick and easy production, should be looked upon as a matter of course, but which in fact are unknown to a large part of the working people of the country.

If Confiscation, then, can do all this, why should it not be made to supersede all other policies that have been tried, and all those that are now courting public favor, but which, like the rest are based upon unrepublican economic laws, and must end, therefore, like the rest, in failure and disappointment?

With our resources restored to the people, which can be done only through Confiscation, prosperity would diffuse itself throughout the country as easily as the sun scatters its light.

We will now outline, as briefly as we may, what will be the effects of Confiscation, and what Confiscation means. It means the limiting of every individual fortune in the United States to $100,000.

And the excess of every fortune now exceeding that amount to be confiscated and turned into the public treasury. No exceptions to be made as to persons or the thing owned. Money, land, buildings, bonds, stocks, everything - wherever an excess is found, confiscate.

The anarchist! It is justice and the intelligence of the people that these new tyrants dread. The equity of this reform should be evident to every one who knows that this government was originally established for the good of all. And the time has now come when the work commenced in 1776 should be again resumed, and our latest masters got rid of some way or other.

But, it will be asked, will not a fifty times millionaire give employment to as many men as will 500 men with $100,000 each. No. Not even if madam and himself are at home from toadying up and down through Europe in search of a princeling. (Stop this fad of the spoiled darlings of fortune and you stop a leak through which over $1,000,000,000 of American money has already disappeared. We will sustain this with facts in its proper place.) One million dollars divided among ten men will do ten times more good than if owned by one man. One million dollars owned by one man is like one million acres owned by one man. He will certainly make some kind of use of his acres, but the very best he can do will be as nothing compared to the use a thousand men or more can make of them. It is the same with a million of money. And an enterprise calling for one million dollars of capital can be carried on just as well if that capital is owned by fifty men, as it could if it is owned by one man. We will have more to say on this point before we are done.

The American millionaire has also the power to squander outside of our own territory that which is much needed in his country. And the thousands in money which he sends to Europe for something to hang on his walls would pay for a much needed improvement in some city or town in the country where the money was made.

The American millionaire is a detriment to his own country any way you take him, although a great many people are thoughtless enough to say that we cannot get along without the millionaire. The capital which he controls will be still here after he is legislated out of office, just as it is when Father Time gathers him in.

He not only injures our country by taking its capital away, but he checks development by tying up the resources which he has got title to. He incloses thousands of acres for a few deer or some such to browse in when the whole should be thrown open, and those in need of homes allowed to settle it. There can be no doubt but what this is a great waste of land when we remember how rapidly those reservations were settled when they were thrown open within the last few years. Those large inclosures may or may not contain land suitable for those in need of homes, but a look through the foothills and mountains of California will show that homes can be made among the rocks and canyons even - when people are forced to it. And it is this power of millionaire to compel us to takes his refuse that we have to do with here, and not with the quality of the land in his game preserves. Strip him of this power and you make the "decoration for his wall." the "deer park," and the "princeling" impossible, and the people will once more have come into their own. Let him retain it and he will soon drive us to beat the bush for game that he himself will bag, as he has already bagged the wealth we produced. Let him retain it, and his sixty miles of fencing may or may not inclose worthless land, but it will not be the land, but the idea represented by the deer inside, that will set us to thinking of the aristocratic parasite and of the pauperism and slavery that is a part of his belongings where-ever he is found. Let him retain it a little while longer, and the soldier, who is steadily working his way on to the scene, will be here, and then the power to help ourselves will be gone, for the grip will be at our throats.

Those who are watching the mighty drama that is slowly unfolding itself on the world's stage of to-day, saw during the strike of last summer with what astounding ease a great people can be subjugated by a few disciplined men. And we no longer labor under the mistake of thinking that because they are our own people they will not shoot to kill. Put your brother - aye, your son - into a uniform, and he needs but the word to snuff you out as quick as he would a red handed Apache. He has been drilled to believe that he himself would be snuffed out if he disobeyed. And this result of disobedience is ever present with the man in uniform, and has been engraved into his very soul, for his only God is the drum-head court-martial. This is the creature that has made the aristocratic parasite a fixture in Europe, and he is all that is needed to make the same curse a fixture in our own country, and every attempt to increase his number should be resisted with all the means in our power, until the plunder he is wanted to guard shall have found its way back to its rightful owners.

IV.

We will now show how the principle of Confiscation should work in the case of railroads. This class of property, by the way, should never have been given over to private ownership to begin with. They are for the convenience of the public, just as much as any harbor or navigation ever was. And if it was right that the founders of the Republic should, in the interests of the country's commerce, deny the right of private ownership in our navigable waters, then it was wrong to concede the right of private ownership in railroads. As for the capital to build them with, it was just as easy to get it for that purpose as it was to get capital to dredge harbors, build lighthouses, build forts or the Stanford University. The first railroad, or even the twentieth, never suggested to the leaders of those times any idea of what this rival of the winds and tides would develop into in a few short years. Individual greed has so little time, to spare from the building of its own nest that politics in the United States, where the common good should be the aim of all legislation, has become a hand-to-mouth affair, and the morrow must shift for itself. Busy hunting for spoil, like our own incompetents of to-day, the legislators of the past cared nothing for the morrow; and, without knowing what they were doing really, surrendered a principle to the railroad projectors that was but a spark at the time, but which has spread until we find the blaze devouring us to-day. The statecraft that never found time to look beyond the ringing of the curfew bells would have starved to death had it to compete with those who were then working the lobby, while it was splitting hairs over the Constitution and accepting the "stuff" that would do it "the most good." No class of property shows the justice, and therefore the need, of Confiscation as much as railroads. No class of property has done as much toward absorbing and transferring the whole country into the hands of a comparatively few men as railroads. But when Confiscation gets through with these monarchs of all they survey, the town or section through which these railroads run will not find themselves like a sucked orange by the wayside.

Taking the Southern Pacific Railroad, we find that it runs through Madera County, California, but it is doubtful if ten cents worth of its securities are owned there. Madera County, then, has property within her borders that earns an income, not one cent of which goes to the county where it was earned.[1] The property is there, but the income from it is taken elsewhere. This is the one great flaw in our present economic life, and is the very root of our present troubles.

The income from property is taken from the locality where it was earned. And the farmer's wagon sinks to the hubs for want of money to build good roads. And the laborer is robbed of the income that his labor earned, and he sinks his manhood at the soup-house door. We repeat it: The great defect in our economic life is the taking of the income from the locality where it was earned, and from the laborer, the source of of it all. This does not mean that the laborer must spend his income or wages where it was made. It does not mean that the income from property must be spent in the particular locality where the property is located. It does not mean, in short, that there shall be any restrictions placed upon the individual in any way outside of limiting him to the ownership of $100,000. With that he can do as he likes, and go where he likes - title-hunting if he wishes, when he will be sure to find many bargains, for it is our impression that there will be a slump in that market when the American millionaire is no longer found among the bidders.

To the United States Government must be left the winding up of the affairs of the railroads, and all other paper-represented property, as it is obvious that she can do it much better than the many States of which the country is composed; and the before mentioned excess shall then be turned over to the different counties where the railroads are located, each county to receive in proportion to the value of the railroad property within her limits, and not according to the number of miles.

President Huntington does not own all the stocks and bonds of the Southern Pacific, but for illustration sake we will assume that he does. Is it not plain then that Confiscation, when it gets through with this railroad owner, will have made the counties where it is located its owners, both of the property itself and the income which it earns? Is this Government ownership of railroads? That term as now understood means buying the railroad, and it is the millionaire we are trying to get rid of, but he is still here if you take his railroads and give him something better. We have already said that private ownership should not have been allowed, and we would now confiscate them without any reservation whatever if it were not for the thousands of small investors in their securities and as these small investors must not be injured, we are compelled to leave the railroads in the hands of private owners, as buying out even these small owners would cause a national debt such as we had better steer clear of. But it is not essential to the welfare of the people that the Government should own the railroads. The point we wish to bring out is, that the wealth and resources of the country has found lodgment in a few hands, whereas it should be scattered among all the people, and as long as they are getting the benefit it will matter little to them whether they own it in their Governmental capacity or as individuals, and the counties even are not to hold on to the forfeited excess, but must dispose of it as fast as the people are able to buy.

But Huntington not owning all the securities of the railroad of which he is president, we send for persons and papers and confiscate as fast as the excess turns up, and distribute as described above. "Oh my! Oh my!" comes a voice from out of the woods. "Is not this robbery?" No; nor armed revolution either, but a peaceable solution of the question. Who owns this earth anyway?

When persons and papers are sent for, and one of the interrogated is found to possess, say, $100,000 in money and securities, $100,000 of real estate, and $100,000 of other good things the right of choice Should be given him as to the $100,000 he wishes to retain. For the limiting of every individual fortune to $100,000 does not mean $100,000 of one kind of property and $100,000 of another kind, etc., but $100,000 all told.

Those of our own country are, of course, amenable to our laws, but many of the securities of the road under consideration are owned abroad, and persons and papers there are not responsive to our subpoenas. If it brings disaster to a country to lose income made there, are we not close to one of the causes of the wretched want that is confined to no section of this land as we draw nearer to the man abroad, who is fattening from income that is drawn from all over this country?

Repudiation is unnecessary here. Simply stop the interest on all American securities owned out of the country.

This we have a perfect right to do, and when it is done the foreign holders will be on their way here as fast as the first ship can take them. The despised steerage and all will be full of him.

Here we are once more obliged to use a word that is as hateful to us as it must be to every one who has probed the wounds of this bleeding country in the hope of finding their cause. And probe where we will, and how we will, it is Bonds; always Bonds - the interest bearing bonds. And standing around are the hyena million-aires, from far and near, lapping their income from the dying form whose first breath was the immortal Declaration.

Gas Bonds, Water Bonds, Sugar Bonds, Flour Bonds, Telegraph Bonds,
Railroad Bonds, Bonds, Bonds, Bonds.

School District Bonds, Road Bonds, Municipal Bonds, County Bonds, State Bonds, and United States Bonds - chief offender among them all, whose issue is left to the sweet will of one man - the political freak now in the White House.

[1] The railroad, of course, pays taxes to the county, but it would have to pay taxes even if it had no income.

- (V. editor)

But we always get the money when the foreigner gets the bonds. That is a lie. Here is some sample evidence of it.

When our parasite hears of another large jewel reaching London from the African mines, he says he must have it for madam's tiara, and taking a small matter of $500,000 or so of securities, he goes over, and when we next see him the securities are gone. But has he money in their place? None whatever. Madam's tiara is safe, but this country is not one cent of money the richer by the transaction.

And when it is time for a husband for Miss Parasite, the two old birds start over with bulging grip to get a mate for the sweet damsel - for she is sweet, as they all are, bless them, whether they belong to the millionaire's brood or to the laborer's - and it freezes our blood when we think of what is sure to happen if the dread machine gets to work here as it did over the way - to get, we say, a mate for the damsel, and when he is found there must be money down and this money is obtained in exchange for the bonds, and remains in the same country where the bonds and titles are.

This has been a losing transaction all round, for, alas, the dear one herself goes over in a few days, and when we next hear of her she will be calling on her big brother to go and thrash the whelp that our money purchased.

It does not look like business to make purchases abroad with income producing property. But when they buy, say $50,000,000 of government bonds at a clip, as did the late Wm. H. Vanderbilt, they turn the interest as fast as it comes in into more income producers, and this leaves their cash-till comparatively empty, so that when they need money quick, for there is much competition among this gentry, as in the case of a big jewel or a princeling, they have no option but to be up and away, and our securities being pie to them over there they grab a lot, and then the rush begins.

Nevertheless there must not be the semblance of injustice done to these foreign investors in our securities when they arrive here to make terms. We have the right to stop the interest, but the securities themselves we must redeem. But redeeming them all at once in gold being out of the question, and as that is the only kind of coin that is now acceptable to the foreigners, they must either wait until we get enough of gold, or until they think better of silver, and are willing to take that metal in part payment, and in the meantime while they are making up their mind, about it they must accept the best we are able to give them, namely non-interest bearing bonds.

It is against the grain to bring the unsavory Bond on to the boards again. But looking at him closely, as he now appears, You will notice that he is well broken and as we have no better we must use him to bring in the rest of the untamed band to which he once belonged. Neither should our visitors complain about this form of payment. If all of our obligations from abroad were paid in coin, assuming that we had enough, it would fill Europe with idle money, and as we have always been a good customer, and always prompt in our payments, they should be reasonable, and admit that it is no worse to have idle bonds than it is to have idle money, so long as final payment is assured. Neither should they expect, par value for what did not, in many cases, cost them fifty cents on the dollar. We will pay them market value no more. And do not imagine that these people have been kept waiting very long to find out these terms. For so positive are these leeches, here and elsewhere, of being able to maintain their hold that those we have just finished with will not make a move to come here until the New Bill of Human Rights has become the law of the land.

And this foreigner whom we are done with, so far as his power to injure us goes, is the counterpart of our own millionaire, and the scowl with which he leaves these shores means another crunch of the iron heel on the necks of his own slaves, and it is only the magnitude of the work that is before us, which none but the blind will deny, in the subduing of our own masters, that makes it a sad necessity to refuse aid to the oppressed the world over. One thing is certain however: whether Bunker Hill led to the fall of the Bastile or not, the liberation of the slave in the New World will show way to his liberation in the Old, and in this way do we render him a service, even if we cannot see our way to help him in any other.

-

The foregoing should make plain how the principle of Confiscation will work in the case of railroads, and all other paper-represented property that can be, and is, owned elsewhere than where the property itself is found.

And there is no need of interfering with or changing any of the functions of the different branches of our Government in order to make Confiscation a part of our organic law any more than there would be to increase the duty on imported wool and to collect it. The machineries of the law making, judicial, and executive branches of our Government, are sufficient for any calls that Confiscation can make on them. Any other construction that may be put on what has been said heretofore or may be said hereafter, is all error. If insisted on, what then? Have we run up against the impassable? It is sufficient to say that what is ours is ours to change when the need is evident, and the Constitution itself is not, an exception to the truth of this.

The laws regulating the rising and the setting of the sun are not of our creating, and we cannot hasten or retard its coming and going one iota of time, and we do not live in the age when it could be done.

But the Constitution is a man-made thing, and when growth has made it a straight jacket then the time for ripping has come.

VI.

Once more resuming our pursuit of the millionaire whom we have dispossessed of his railroad plunder, we find the chase taking us into town, where Confiscation will find many problems which it alone can solve - where it will find his sixteen story building, for his hours of plotting, and his suburban palace for his hours of ease, and the hiving humanity between over whom he had to walk to reach either. Those palaces on the Nob hills of these United States are the toadstools of the decay that is going on in this Republic to-day.

The master crime of all ages was the building of those pyramids on the Egyptian sands, for they were useless, but the whim and the slaves and the lash of power were there, and the pyramids went up.

Let us see to it that the power of our pyramid builders is destroyed before it gets beyond five million dollar palaces.

-

When we apply the principle of Confiscation to the millionaire merchant and turn his excess into the public treasury, it will be no more destructive of the business of which he has had all the profits than it was of the railroads. There will be more business done in the same line than ever, but more will be doing it, and consequently more will share in the profits. But if our object is to break up these fabulous fortunes, which mean certain death to our liberties, and whose blight has paralyzed progress and development, there should be no reason why we should not allow the present owners to take a hand in the breaking up. If the merchant, or other millionaire, would rather divide his millions among his relatives (barring his wife and minors) and friends, than to resign it over to the public treasury, let him do so. Our aim will be attained whichever happens, which is simply to bring about a better distribution of the wealth of this country, and we know of no way of making this even distribution that will compare with Confiscation. Socialism, in all its forms, means the surrendering of individual liberty, and is a retrograde movement, and the outcome of it can be nothing more or less than despotism of the very worst kind.

Socialism enlarges the power of one individual over another. This is incompatible with the liberty that goes with a republic. Confiscation says, $100,000 is enough. When you are found with more, it will be considered as proof that you have been taking an unfair advantage of some one, and the surplus makes you dangerous to the welfare of a republic, and is therefore forfeited. There will be nothing more disagreeable, so far as the right of the individual goes, in the enforcing of this proposed law than there is in the collection of taxes on incomes. Cutting a fortune down to the $100,000 limit may be considered a very disagreeable thing indeed, but when we are reminded that it is all done for the common good, we become reconciled at once, for we feel in our heart of hearts that the altar at which we can cheerfully make whatever sacrifices we are called upon to make, is the altar of our brother's welfare.

The millionaire merchant will doubtless take advantage of his right to divide his business among his relatives and friends. Naturally they would give him the management, but the instinct to be master is strong within us all, and this would soon break up and scatter that dangerous accumulation. Then there would be more Market streets and Broadways. Every dollar of business that would be taken from the one or two principal thoroughfares, which is all that is now found in any of the cities, would mean an increase of value in the property of the street where this transfer business is carried on. And this increase in the value of city property would continue on out to the city's limits; and the limits themselves would be extended further out to find room for habitable homes for the human beings that are supposed to live in the tenements. There can be no question but what merchandising would spread itself more over the cities if this limited ownership of capital was in force; and this spreading out will give employment to all in bringing about the change; and prosperity, such as goes with plenty of work, will take the place of the wretched misery and want that now fill all the soup-house infected cities of the country. There will be no impairment in the value or need of the big "dailies" that are published in these centres of population. They will simply be owned by more people and read by more, and the improvement in the times being of a stable and permanent character their circulation will be free from the rise and fall with which they are now only to well acquainted, and the cheap-John business into which so many have gone, in the last few years, wheedling the ten cents and the dollars out of the child-like poor for worthless truck, can be thrown into the waste basket with the last offer of money for a Wall Street editorial. It is a mistake, by the way, to think we are a nation of readers. Man is an interesting animal where-ever found, the desire to know what he has done and is doing is strong in us all, but even the little county paper is beyond the reach of many. The writer, who is a common toiler like the rest, finds the moving world a sealed book to him, for he cannot spare the needed dollar, and live. And those editors who will fiercely rend and tear, with all the power of their trained brains and skilled pens, at this vital need of our times may live to see the day when they too will believe this world is round, and that calling the original believers fools, thieves, scoundrels, rascals, and enemies to civilization was a repetition of an old mistake. It will be the day when they can be our guides, philosophers, and friends without the itching palm stuck out behind. It will be the day when we can accept, without doubt or a curl of the lip, the admonition. from the sixteen stories of steel, because we will then know, that the conscience of the man within is not itself all awry.

To whatever cause the existing rot is chargeable the editor, at least of all others, had the power to stop or check it, and failure to meet this great responsibility shows that the strut of this great personage is assumed, and that, like the rest, his necessities have been used by the master to bend and break him till he no longer dare call his soul his own.

We can expect the screech of this helpless tool to fill the land as his desperate master nags him on in the revolution that is coming.

VII.

The mammoth hotel where the parasite of greater or lesser degree sojourns, where the popping corks of the costly imported champagne is heard, can still be a hotel, but the profits of its millions of invested capital must no longer he taken away by one or two men and it therefore must have many more owners than it has now. It, too, must go to the people, if its millionaire owner can find no more relations to share with and begins to suspect his "friends" of having had a hand in bringing about the upheaval. And if the "plain" people never expect to enjoy the material results of the inventive wit of man as they are focused within its luxurious interior, they at least have some reason for being satisfied when they know that the profits will stay where they were made and help those who made them. This reference to hotels brings to mind a corroborative fact that proves the charge we make when we say that all these colossal fortunes are nothing more than the accumulations of able rascality of some form or other: bilking, cornering, lobbying, watering stock, or charging all the traffic will bear.

The Palace Hotel in San Francisco was built by a speculator and floater of mining shares, and cost millions that he cashed in, after cleaning out the simple minded laborer and servant girl, whom he deluded, with all the art known to his tribe, into believing that there was still more for their rainy day if they would only invest the little they already had.

The law makes a felon of the rascal with the bogus gold brick, but that clumsy worker in the field of robbery does not get the returns which the scienced work of his brother professional brings in; therefore, when outraged law gives this petty malefactor the knock-out blow, the satisfied spectators, chattering about the majesty of something, depart and the curtain is rung down on another exhibition of what the American people are said to like - namely, humbug. Let us say in passing, that the American does not like humbug. Take the average of him as he is found in the little world in which the routine work of his life is done and you will find him alert and close enough to deal with, and that in all things in which he has his experience to rely on humbug (swindling) is practically impossible. But when he gets outside of that experience, then, like the experienced traveler, he patiently submits to imposition when resistance might mean a loss greater than the original. But even the traveler must have enough to continue on with, and when imposition reaches that stage resistance begins. So it will be with the man who is said to like humbug (robbery), when he finds humbug (slavery) closing in on him. He too will resist. He did before and the rightful owners gained possession, as this same man, who is said to like humbug, will again recover possession of what is being so stealthily taken from him.

When outraged law is asked to administer justice to the scoundrel who has deluded thousands into buying worthless mining shares or some such swindling bait, the victims are told that the whole swindle has been legitimized by the great seal of the state, and that their loss is the profits of a business conducted by a licensed trader.

The man with the bogus gold brick goes to jail. The man with the bogus gold mine goes free.

Why this difference when the principle in the two crimes is the same? Is it because the millionaire swindler has, in fact, been given rights under the law that is denied to the smaller fry? Or is it because the larger bird of prey makes enough to go all around? Certain it is, however, that Labor in its contests with Capital never got a decision in its favor yet - in time to be of any service.

These wholesalers found the concubining of justice herself a necessity to the success of their rascalities and the delays and decisions of this harlot are but the echoes of her paramour's orders. And at no time does the debasement of this whited sepulchre display itself more than when the miserable and friendless criminal whose crime is, assuredly, nothing more than the natural and to be expected outcome of the wrong and inexcusable crime developing conditions under which he is compelled to live, is at her altar for Justice, which She renders in ringing tones such as are never heard when Her paramour or his hirelings are before Her.

When Labor does finally get a decision it is as worthless to it as is its pass-book on the gutted savings bank.

Make the millionaire an extinct species, and the above assertion will not have logic to sustain it, and our courts will not be making terrible "examples" of the friendless, while the thief who ruins thousands is allowed to go free.

-

There must be a radical change made in our laws if we ever expect to stop the sharks from preying on us. Our laws, like a hole in a fence, makes access easy, and the endless raids will never cease until the holes are stopped up. Constant watching, even with the light from former experiences, will all count for nothing while those holes and breaks are left open. The persistent work of the crew of sharpers that has the Nicaragua canal steal in tow shows this necessity for a change in the economic laws of the country. Duplicating the scheme by which the Huntingtons and Oakes Ameses robbed the people they submitted their prospectus for endorsement, and, lo, this whole coast grovels in the dust to these new Moseses, who are to show them the way out of the wilderness into which their original, Huntington, has led them.

The canal should be built. But the estimated cost of the whole enterprise was $66,000,000 according to their own expert, whose report, eight years ago, was published in "Harper's Weekly" - (published as news, by the way, but was an advertisement, and paid for as such. And that Julian Ralph stuff that appeared in that same weekly lately is more of that peculiar kind of news that is being constantly ground out by the capitalistic sharks to catch the unwary, and was paid for by Spreckels - another Moses, that has come to the succor of our beleaguered coast. The "Journal of Civilization" is a fit organ for the millionaire corruptionist and the civilization that he is degrading) - and although they have gone over the ground again and again since that report was made, the maximum estimate is still well inside $100,000,000. Yet they now want to issue $100,000,000 in stock; want the people to guarantee principal and interest on $70,000,000 of bonds, and the right to issue $30,000,000 of bonds themselves. No wonder it was called a steal on the floor of the Senate. The public treasury will ever be the objective point of such wholesalers until the inducement is removed. Humanity, Honor,

Patriotism, each and all are powerless before this all conquering appetite of Individual Greed.

What can such people as they care for this people, their country and its benign form of government? What use have such as they for a government that denies them the title that distinguishes their kind over the sea?

Ay, what is to prevent them from using the vast power that goes with the wealth they are absorbing day by day, and to gratify the one unsatisfied wish of their purse-proud and selfish souls, and establish an Empire in place of the Republic? The Republic is but a shell and their work would be easy.

The sophistry about the inalienable right of one man to crush another has had its day, and their hypocritical wail about civilization and this inalienable right, when these conscienceless rascals find their race is run, will be like the yelling of remorseless wolves that have been trapped and kicked into the vanishing distance.

VIII.

Understanding the principle of Confiscation, it will be easily seen how it must work in every individual case; and, therefore, it is needless to dwell on or elaborate its workings when it is applied to banks, breweries, sugar refineries, water works, gas works, street railways, etc.

It will not destroy capital or business. It may lessen the value of real estate on the principal streets in large cities, and fall in values is not certain even there. It will trouble no one, however, if it does; not the present owner, even, for the value of property in favored localities is so great now that, however much one man can own now, he can own but a fraction of it under the proposed change. The owner of, say, a $400,000 building and lot on such a street as we are now considering may find a shrinkage of $100,000. This will give him two partners instead of three. The shrinkage, therefore, will be to his liking; for, be it known, the aristocrat is a proud bird, and likes to flock by itself. And any designs against these two partners will be so fruitless of results to himself that a word in his ear now and then by his friends and well-wishers, about the public treasury, will end in his cultivating, such a lamblike submission to the new dispensation that his eloquence, born of the new light and an awakened conscience, will make his titled sister over the way give up her bauble when he shows her the cost of its pomp to the struggling poor.

Such will be the effect of the change on a man who now carries the law in his pocket, when he hasn't it under his feet.

Moving the laborer so far away from the centre of the city, and where there is room to build habitable homes, will be a serious objection, it will be urged. They cannot get to their work on time without getting up at all hours. They can just have time to snatch a bite and be away again. And the whole of Sunday must be given to sleep they cannot get at any other time.

They will be strangers in the near-by theatre, and the near-by library will be given up to the spider and his web, and the little garden of flowers that the once half-starved women have made a delight will be unknown to the worn out bread-winner, who will be the same old slave we premised to unshackle. Better clothes surely, and his home shows what it is to be a citizen of a republic that is a republic in fact as well as in name; but he has only time to snatch a bite and be away again.

Will it never occur to those critics that we are here dealing with the greatest creation of the Almighty, and of all time - civilized man; and that we must make the conditions fit him, and not he the the conditions.

Everything he eats, wears, and uses in twelve months can be produced in two. Why, then, should he be compelled to labor twelve months for that which can be produced or made in one-sixth of that time? The reason is plain. When two laborers make an exchange there is wholesale robbery committed by the non-producing and idle parasites, while the fruits of Labor are on the way to those who alone are entitled to the whole. "And I," says the millionaire, "say this robbery must go on, for I am an impossibility without it." That gnawing canker never had any doubts as to where his surfeit comes from. And now that it has become a question of life and death with those he has been plundering, he should be dragged to the bar of justice and compelled to disgorge. And then labor, too, can come in on the eight and nine o'clock train, and be no later for its work than is the banker and the rest of his class that have had Labor under their heels so long.

The capacity of the modern world to produce has entirely outstripped her capacity to consume, and trying to solve the economic problems of the day, by further denial or ignoring of this fact, that should be self-evident, will be to build a structure with only half the foundation laid, and the inevitable collapse is bound to follow.

There will always he plenty of room in the heart of a city for those who must live close to their work.

But the inventor has made night work, except by the parasitical leeches, unnecessary to the masses, a few hours of daylight being more than sufficient to supply all the needs of the country. We are not insisting, be it understood, on a four-hour or eight-hour system of labor. No industry or occupation will be hampered or meddled with by doing justice to the laborer in the way proposed. The railroad employee, printer, baker, factory hand, etc., can work on as now, but they must be compensated with just wages for the labor done. This will enable them to retire before decrepitude comes on, and orders are left for the poorhouse ambulance to call on its way out.

If every city occupied three times the ground they now do, they would be gainers in all ways, and the moral degradation into which large sections of them have sunk would disappear with the conditions that produced them.

The capacity of Europe to feed her people is being crowded, we are told, and then our flag is again run-up, and during the whole exhibition the Chinese system of bunking is quietly fastening itself in every city of consequence in the country. When those sorely pressed people, whose very existence is being threatened by these foreigners of a degraded civilization, awaken to the extremity of their danger, the bunking system and its introducers will find perjury and the habeus corpus mill powerless to save them. Mark this, however. The big capitalist imported the Chinaman, and his powerful influence has defeated all attempts to remove him. It follows, then, that we must break up the big capitalist, if we ever expect to get at the thing behind him.

We are not indifferent to the hardships of the oppressed of other nations, but we cannot get out of our own perplexities by saying that we are more favored in some way than are others. There are rocks ahead of ourselves, and watching others going to pieces and firing congratulatory guns will not help them or save us from, a like fate.

Whatever is in the near future for Europe, we, at least, have nothing to fear as to the capacity of our country to support all her people. And as it is with room for producing, so it is with room in which to live. There is plenty of both, and we should show ourselves worthy of the legacy left us by that handful of brave men who established liberty in our country, and insist on getting plenty of both before the armed hireling appears and it is too late.

IX.

We will now apply the principle of Confiscation to land, and we will see that Confiscation alone can undo the wrong that has of late become apparent to even the law makers in Washington. Up to within three years or so there were two ways by which farming lands could be obtained from the Government - by homesteading and preempting.

It is unnecessary to give the laws of either, but so fast was this class of land going that Congress repealed the preemption law. In other words, the amount you could obtain was cut down one half - from 320 acres to 160. What was more significant still of their barn door work after the horse was gone, they made the owning of 160 acres, regardless from whom it was got, private purchase or Government, a bar to the taking up of Government farm land. Prior to the repeal every citizen, and those intending to become citizens, had certain land rights, and owning half a State did not impair them; which all goes to show that even this free and easy-going Government thought it about time to call a halt. But that was all it did do. As it was not necessary to give the laws under which the homesteader and preemptor got title, neither is it necessary to here ask how some men became owners of all the way from 1,000 to 60,000 acres, every acre of which was Government land years after California became a State. (We are using California facts. The rest of the Western part of the United States has an abundance of the same kind.) Suffice it to say, that they now own them; and suffice it too, that Confiscation is the only way by which we can dispossess them of plunder, that the welfare of the country demands should be returned? In Confiscation alone will the people find a servant who will not condone the past, but will follow up this breed of the grabber and restore what it finds, as it has already done with others of his tribe.

It will be the re-discovering of America.

Never did kind and beneficent laws show what men, with the right kind of stuff in them, could do, as did our land laws. Men who now own territory as large as some of the Eastern States started in without a dollar. They had something better. They had consciences that was good for any tests that the scoundrels could put them to. Never did gangs of "floaters" help the political boss and ward-heeler rob the public treasury with greater success than did this other brand of the bastard citizen help his boss to hog the public domain.

In the fertile valley of the Sacramento, land that would give one hundred and sixty acre homes to ten thousand families (fifty thousand people) is owned by one hundred individuals, all average of sixteen thousand acres to each owner. This is but a fraction of the valley and leaves out the owners of less than sixteen thousand acres.

In the great San Joaquin valley, the laborer in search of work can walk for days in one direction alongside of fencing that incloses land belonging to one firm. And this immense fortune-in land was obtained by robbery, just as the other millionaire fortunes were obtained.

In the land office we see the miserable tool and his master.

In the legislative halls we see the miserable tool and his master.

And we see the leaves on Liberty's Tree droop and wither as these deadly borers do their work under the bark below.

Up among the peaks and valleys of the Sierra Nevada lies the town of Mariposa, settled by gold seekers whose rich findings gave world wide fame to this hamlet among the mountains. Aluvial gold and quartz bearing gold was scattered with lavish hand through the surrounding hills, and in the beds of the summer-dried streams. Generous laws of their own making, gave ample room, and the eager workers toiled on, forgetting the past hardships of the long journey where so many fell by the way, and the rugged hills became endeared to them as they marked out the shaded spots on their shelving sides where their coming dear ones could look down on the busy scene below. But the camp follower with ready knife never finished the wounded brave quicker than did the "land grant" swindler finish Mariposa when her riches became the theme of every gold camp throughout the world. And to-day the big hearted and stalwart miner goes to fever-laden Africa and ice-bound Alaska, when there are whole mountains of the best mineral bearing land in the world in his own country, but which our present laws forbid him to touch.

Our people should no more bow to a Mexican land grant title than to a superstition of their cave-dwelling ancestors.

What matters it, however, in what way these colossal robberies were committed; by coffee-stained lie from Mexico, or perjured oath of faithless citizen; it has been done, and it is time for the undoing.

Man developed the school house, and for this each is indebted to the other, and the mutual debt is acknowledged by making the school free to all.

The Creator developed the Earth from chaos to the habitable home of man, free to all, but this debt is not acknowledged, and the many are driven into the highway by the few.

Give us all the conveniences of modern life, railroads, telegraphs, etc., etc., etc., but give us back the land, that is our natural heritage as much as is the water we drink or the air we breath.

Give us back this birthright, or take your railroads, and so on, and your civilization, and sink them deep in the depths of hell, for the starving have no use for them, and we'll take the savage state that knows no hunger except in the time of famine.

X.

Limit the ownership of land, be it arable, grazing, timber, or any other kind, to 160 acres. As no one shall own more than $100,000 worth of property all told, this 160 acres will have to be reduced as we get near to the centres of population. This will still give the owner of such convenient land an advantage over those living further out, who will always be willing to exchange should the first rather follow the coarser grades of farming to dairying or gardening.

Neither is there any reason why the owning of great sections of timber land by one or two men should be necessary to the running of sawmills and supplying the people with lumber. The mills are capable of doing just as good work if the fifty quarter sections are owned by fifty men as they are if owned by one man. And the waste of timber seen on every hand wherever you find a mill owned and operated by capitalists would have been unknown if there had been an individual owner to each quarter section. The wanton waste of this breed of the capitalist, in his hurry to pile up, would have been impossible had his mill been a "custom" mill, to saw the timber from your quarter section and mine instead of his fifty or five hundred. And the poor unskilled laborer would not have to go to make room for the chinaman, or that member of a worthless tribe who sold his "claim" to the "company" for so much and the promise of a job. The small owner cannot afford the waste of the large one. His income will not be so great that he can afford to waste the principal from which it comes. As to any friction about whose turn it is to run his timber through, it is only necessary to say that the business will be then carried on by those who are now doing the labor, and it will be no worse to accept wages from the man on the neighboring claim for helping him to make lumber than it was to accept wages from the man who was dethroned, and he will probably pay you as much as you could make running your own logs through.

If this is not satisfactory, sell out at once to one of the many that are waiting to buy, and go, for you will not find anything in what we are advocating that interferes in the least with the liberty of the individual. Some may think differently, but then they are the ones who brought all eyes to the window to see what was going on in the street.

And as you travel on you will miss the once eager dog at the farm house by the way, and no palsied hand will be lifting the corner of the curtain as you are passing by, for the tramp has disappeared, and the rare survivor and incurable will be doing it on bread and water, for he must be a useless thing not to have drawn his last breath with his compatriot at the other end of the scale.

The farmer who has children that are not of age when the new arrangement goes into force will see great hardship in the 160-acre law. He intended to give this piece of land to one son and that piece to another, and so on. He would give each of these sons more, but some one else owns the rest of the country thereabouts, and these, say, 160-acre tracts, are the best he can do. Leaving out of the question whether his sons can locate alongside of himself or not, and confining ourselves to their chance of being able to get 160 acres, which is the vital point in the whole matter, he must see that, if he must surrender his excess and all others must do the same, there would be more land to take up than there are people to take it. We are in a Republic, Mr. Farmer, and the interest of the many who have called at your door call on you to disgorge with the rest.

When we come to the land in the mountains we find that it averages poor, yet the 160-acre law must be applied there also. To allow more would be to give an opening to the smart one, who would take advantage as he has always done; and as the country is pretty well tired of him we will save future complications by tying him down to 160 acres like the rest. The mountain farmer or rancher, with rare exceptions, gets his income from the raising of pork or beef animals, which are rarely confined to the owner's premises, but are allowed to roam and graze where they will, at times as far as forty and fifty miles away from where they belong. And as the mountaineer makes little if any provisions for the barn feeding of his animals, outside of one or two milk cows and his few work animals, and these last only through the work season and the bad weather of whatever winter the locality may have, he will not find his business of raising meat for the market curtailed in any respect.

Should he need more hay or grain ground, or ground for orchards or gardens, be will always find it inside of his 160-acre inclosure, for there are none yet among them who knows the possibilities of a 160-acre ranch under the plow. And as none has yet been forced to put the plow into outside ground, it can be taken for granted that they never will.

Where, then, is the reason why this class of farmers should be allowed title to more land than the others? The range or grazing ground among the hills and along the water courses will still be open to their animals, and instead of the proposed change injuring their business, it will, in these days of cheap barb-wire, stop the would-be cattle king and speculative grabber from crippling or destroying it altogether, a fate not unknown to some who have tried in a small way to make a living from cattle raising.

There is, therefore, no reason why the farmer in the hills should be allowed more land than his less favored brother in the valleys and plains below. He must fall into line with the rest; and, as he takes his place at the foot the assembled multitude of liberated slaves, sees a gleam of scorn in the eyes of the once mighty railroad king as this poor relation is thrust upon his notice.

But it is not in a brave people to humiliate a fallen enemy, and the order to break ranks is given, and the ex-slave and ex-master mingle together, and depart to work out a destiny common to both.

-

In the preceding pages we have briefly tried to show that Confiscation is the only peaceable way that is now open to us by which the people can again obtain possession of their country. And we have tried to convey an idea of how its principle should be applied, and we will now turn our attention to its workings, and show, as briefly as possible, how easy it is for the people to be prosperous when they have control of their country's resources.

There is not a railroad in the country that would not be taxed to its utmost in carrying settlers to the forfeited lands; and the work of the land agent and boomer, the uphill work of the town or section in trying to build themselves up by advertising far and near, and the hauling of cars full of exhibition pumpkins crossways and lengthways of the land, would be needless. Government land, be it County, State or United States, never requires booming in these days of the anxious home-seeker, and never will again.

At present when a new section becomes attractive there is a rush into it, and then the rush slacks up with an air-brake suddenness. The speculator has got there and pitched his tent, and his $100 to $500 acre signs - part down, the rest at 8 per cent. - has taken possession, and the stream is turned aside and goes elsewhere. And then the pumpkin, with its 8 per cent. tags plastered all over it, is put aboard and hauled through the country on its mission of deceiving the innocent.

With the land speculator out of the way, and no expenses outside of office fees, there would be a steady increase of population wherever there is agricultural land, until the last acre is in possession of an actual settler, whose home would be on the place. (The principle which allows a man living in New York, or somewhere else, to own land in California, or somewhere else, should set every law-maker to scratching his head to see if he cannot get an idea out of it.)

And do not plague yourselves about the numerosity of the new settler, and where the whole of him is to find a market. We are trying to get rid of the pauper, and whoever heard of a farm, free of the 8 per cent. night-mare, being the breeding place of such as he? Whatever else happens to the farmer he at least is sure of enough to eat. Wheat may be down; cattle without buyers; eggs a drug; potatoes left to rot in the ground, milk wasting like water, and not ten cents in money on the premises, but the owner is not starving. The dude may not see a brother in him, and he will be denied entrance to the Inner Circle when Major domo McAllister sees him in the rear. But he has weight, and looks as if trying to get away with this year's crop, to make room for the next, agrees with him; and if he thinks now and again of the days of the hungry tramp it must be that the undertaking has proportions he little dreamed of.

But he will have a market. What causes him to need one? This. That he may be able to get that which he does not produce or make himself. And is there not some one else producing or making those very things, and who needs what the farmer alone produces or makes? If yes, then we have found the whole secret of what we call business - two producers or makers of different articles making an exchange one with the other. Stop that exchange, and there would be no manufacturing; we would all be living off raw nature once more, and our ball-games would give way to the pelting of cocoanuts and hanging by our tails.

XI.

The opening of these forfeited lands would be the salvation of that pitiable creature, the victim of the 8 per cent. grind. The homeless wanderer can get shade and shelter from the burning sun and driving storm, and with these is content, for he has long since resigned ambition to those who are willing to continue the hopeless struggle; but the man, on the 8 per cent. treadmill, who has not yet acknowledged defeat, has no way of escape from the glare of the master's eye, except by self-murder or the pauper's grave. There is nothing that excites our hatred against the infamous laws of our times as much as does the sight of this brave man struggling against the fate that is crushing him, and whose patriotism will soon be kindred to that of the Russian serfs, if it does not go to the other extreme and make him a nihilist or some other brand of the political desperado. It was from this quarter, forget it not, that the old flint locks came, "whose report was heard around the world," and the serf will never be his model, for the old spirit has still enough of life left for another blaze, as these new oppressors will find to their awful cost.

The burdens which these people are staggering under can be easily imagined when it is known that they have been paying interest on mortgages for years that the places would not now sell for, even after they were improved by years of labor and the outlay of much money. In the San Joaquin valley, for instance, there are homesteads by the thousands that will not sell for what they are mortgaged for, and the extraordinary spectacle was witnessed in the city of San Francisco last year of a bank having to close because it could not sell out the valley farmers for the mortgages due it. Of course these farmers obtained money from the bank, and the justice of the bank's claim is not what we are now trying to get at, but to show that if we had the laws that belong to a republic the people would not be the victims of bankers or any one else. Had they been allowed in the first place to take possession of all unimproved land without having to give up the savings of years to some land grabber, whose theft was authorized and sustained by law, and then loaded down with interest obligations, they would have had no more trouble in keeping their land than they would in keeping an arm or a leg.

With every one limited to 160 acres there would be so much thrown open to settlement that it would practically wipe out all mortgages on land, for the occupant of mortgaged premises, could give his owner the option of accepting what would be a fair price under the new conditions, and if it were refused then the occupant could simply back his wagon up, put his portables on and drive to some of the Government land nearest to him.

And it should not be so difficult to get the fencing and the lumber for the few small buildings that would answer till he could get better, and, once started, his condition would be a steady improvement, the interest he now pays remaining on the premises where it is made. At present there are the usual fences and buildings put up when the land is bought (part down, the rest at 8 per cent.), and these are the only improvements, outside of vine and tree growth, that can be made; the wear of time even cannot be repaired, for the occupant has nothing to spare for repairs or improvements, and even the necessaries of life are a tug, and as to decent clothing for himself and wife and other dependants that is not to be thought of while he is loaded down with that bane of modern life, interest obligations.

The cost of moderately sized buildings would of course depend on circumstances, but it should not exceed a few hundred dollars; and as it would be a more profitable investment for a county to help a settler, that is already on the ground, to get a start, than to spend the money trying to get him there, as is the practice now, there can be no serious reason why the voters should not authorize their local Government to extend the necessary aid, and make it optional with the borrower whether he shall pay in money or work; the length of time and other details to be governed by circumstances, but no interest to be charged. If this last causes some apparent loss, let it be charged to the old pumpkin fund.

There are people of small means who have taken mortgages on land, and these must be protected, as we have already done in the case of like investors in paper-represented property. But if these small lenders are already owners of one hundred and sixty acres they must make the best terms they can with their debtors, for it is a cardinal idea of this needed readjustment that no one shall own more than 160 acres. But if the lender does not own that amount of land, he can get and hold title as at present.

-

The result of the proposed change being to keep the income of the whole country within its own borders, it follows that every section must find itself with an abundance of capital such as was never known to them before, giving them the means to carry on improvements that are entirely beyond them now. At the present time, too, if a laborer, through errors of judgment, should lose the savings of his years of youth and strength, he can rarely recover the ground lost, and finds that paying his way from day to day thereafter is all he can do, and when his work days are gone for good he must either go to the poor-house or be cared for by his relations, whose own load is about all they can bear up under. With the income kept where it is made all this is would be changed, for then, instead of having work only a part of the time, and poor wages besides, the laborer, when his work for private parties gave out, could get work from the local Government, which always has it to give, and the money to pay for it. And should a laborer here and there through some unforeseen cause, be forced by poverty and age to accept food and shelter that he cannot pay for, his relations can provide for him, for the getting of the mere food and clothing will not be the momentous question that it is now. And this power of the local Government to give work will save many a one from a fate that should never overtake the honest and willing.

Pauperism and crime can never be eliminated from society, any more than the susceptibility to sickness and disease can be eliminated from flesh and blood, but as civilization grows older its accumulating wisdom should be more than a match for poverty, the parent germ of both pauperism and crime; but the discouraging fact is that these two diseases of civilized society are advancing faster than civilization itself, and we build larger poor houses and jails, and then sit down and nurse the hideous disorders, as if they were the incurable rot of leprosy instead of being the result of economic laws that allow the able to rob the weak.

There is not a county or State but what has plenty of work had it the money to do it. The question of good roads is becoming prominent, but if they are ever built under our present system of economics they will be built by slave labor pure and simple. It is absolutely out of the question for the people to raise the money for running the Government; pay interest on bonds; pay for the bonds themselves; pay pensions; carry on the costly work of giving the whole country macadamized roads, and care for the millionaire, and remain free at the same time.

Government expenses.

Pensions.

Interest on bonds.

Matured bonds.

Macadamized roads.

Care of millionaire.

To think of carrying such a load and remain free is madness.

We are contending that the country is already crushed with debt; that she is saddled with such a tremendous load, that, like the mortgaged farm, improvement and progress is utterly out of the question. We have the resources for any and every improvement that the country needs, but they are wasted and squandered paying interest to foreign capitalists, and supporting our mushroom growth of millionaire parasites, who are the cause of our poverty of capital, and the foreigners' ability to lend us money.

Do away with interest paying and the millionaire, and the required roads could be commenced at once, and as for the Nicaragua canal, we would make as light of it as does the farmer in hoeing a hill of beans.

XII.

The silver interest asserts that we will never stop our headlong rush to the devil if we do not get free coinage of silver. Silver, like pork or potatoes, is something for sale, and its owners have given up their whole attention to finding it a market. Whoever heard of J. P. Jones interesting himself in anything except silver. Never in all of his twenty years of public life did he show that he was anything more than "a man from one of the Silver States." Ever and always whenever he fills the air with his noise, you have only to look and there you will find him still knocking at the public treasury for a customer that already has had enough of him.

He has become a monomaniac on silver, and, although one of the principal owners of the Mariposa land grant, will not open it up because it is silver he wants and the grant only shows gold. It is this dementia that secures him a life-lease of the Senatorship from Nevada. For Nevada has only one interest, and that is silver. Silver is her wool, her cotton, her wheat, her coal, her iron, her lumber, her manufactures. It made her a State. It made her first representative to Congress and her last. It made Jones - Jones the drummer whose one sample is silver, who talks of silver, who sings of silver, who dreams of silver, and who gets his inspirations of the past, present, and future as he looks down the shaft of his silver mine in Nevada.

Never did the tail of the dog work harder than does this little bob-tailed thing called silver, that we find moving around among our legs, trying to trip us up every time the political procession makes a move.

There is distress because there is not money enough in circulation, say these peddlers of silver. It is a well understood fact that every sound bank in the country has idle money in its vaults looking for investment.

Money is precisely like the laborer - it, too, is on the lookout for work. Show money where it can make interest, and it will come out of those vaults as quick as the hungry laborer will answer the knock at his door.

Whatever distress the laborer is suffering, however, be sure that the millionaire owner of that idle money feels it not. His belly is well filled and his back well covered, and he knows nothing of the jolt of the box-car as he listens to the rhythm of the wheels of his Pullman sleeper. And it matters little to this millionaire, this flower of a foreign clime, when his increase sets in again. He has millions, a word we little comprehend the meaning of, and he will never know distress, any more than the laborer will know plenty again while this vampire of progress is permitted to survive. But the time must come when labor will get to work again for a few months each year, the usual thing now, to produce the needed stock of necessaries for the country, and then he will see the man of millions step off and collect his usual toll, and enough besides to make good any shrinkage in the principal. This owner of immense capital, this traveler in the Pullman, who makes his regular rounds through the country collecting toll off every laborer in every section, preparatory to his flight to Europe, is twin brother to the great land owner, and there is no hope for our country until both are legally or otherwise exterminated.

-

We could undo the capitalist by making interest illegal, as this would force him. to draw on his principal. We do not object, however, to the interest capital receives. Banks have no enemy in this proposed change, and we suspect either the motives or the judgment of those whose stock in trade is a howl against banks, and what they call usury. Money has its place in civilization, and the bank where it is dealt in is a shop just as much as is the dry goods store or grocery, and is entitled to its profits just the same. If a man earns $5,000 he should be allowed to charge something for its use the same as for the wagon be made or the house he built. Neither the wagon nor house is any more the result of his labor than is this money, and no one will question his right to charge something for the use of the first two. It is here where the banks are of service - the man with money takes it to a place - the bank - where the man who wishes to hire it knows where to look for it. Good sense will not deny a market to a man with potatoes; neither will it deny him a market for any other product of his labor, be it capital or what not. Interest is wrong only when it is being drawn by a millionaire, who, of course, did not earn the principal. Those millions is where the danger lies, when found with an individual owner, whether they are in bank vaults or on the shelves of the millionaire merchant. Besides, it is a slow process, this breaking up the millionaire owner of some thing by stopping his interest. This earth should be ours while we are alive to enjoy it, and there is no hope of getting it by applying the graduated tax idea to either land or capital. When a curse like poverty can be removed the quicker it is done the better.

Interest is wrong (we are not justifying extortion) when it is drawn by the millionaire, not only because his labor did not earn the principal, but because he has the power to take it out of the country where it was earned. And he does take it out thereby impoverishing the country of the capital that is needed to carry on developments that should never be allowed to stop.

There is, as has been said, idle money now, but the millionaire owners care nothing for the general welfare, and the people cannot get this idle money because they find it impossible to pay interest for its use, and carry at the same time the fearful burdens they are now loaded with.

An individual can be forced to submit to any kind of terms when his necessities are driving him. When those necessities are satisfied he must stop and let development go, for he cannot stand the terms. He is willing to go ahead, but he simply finds his physical being unequal to the task. As it is with one individual so it is with a nation of individuals. They also can be forced to submit to any kind of terms when their necessities are driving them, and when their necessities are supplied they too must stop and let development go, for they cannot stand the terms. In other words, the capacity of people, singly or collectively, is limited, and if they are compelled to exhaust that capacity in supporting millionaire parasites at home, and paying for their extravagance abroad, they cannot improve themselves or develop their country.

Complicity, then, and negligence on the part of our law makers has made a few men the absolute owners of the financial or money branch of our economics, and the people find it impossible to move except when these masters find it to their interests to let them.

Progress under such conditions will never be more than a dream.

We could find use for all the capital that is now in the country, and all that has been and is being taken out of it, but we should first loosen the grip of these legalized despoilers and see how far what we have got would go before we talk of issuing more, which would soon turn up missing like the rest.

XIII.

We hear much about what we are losing by the balance of trade being against us, but not a word about that other floodgate through which our capital is rushing, namely, our millionaire class making its purchases abroad, and their other expenses while living among the foreign birds of a like feather. Their idle money is left here for investment. They do not look to that quarter for income. The world over there is under the feet of a few as it is here, and the result is the same - idle money looking for interest.

No less an authority than the late Ward McAllister has said that up to last year two hundred and eighty American women had married foreign titles.

$1,000,000,000 was the war indemnity demanded of France by the Germans, and so vast is this sum that the civilized world believed the Germans wanted to retain possession of the conquered country and demanded what the French could not pay. Yet the amount of American money it took to buy those two hundred and eighty titles is far in excess of that war indemnity. At four millions each it would exceed $1,000,000,000. But the average cost must have been more than four millions. One of our millionaire flour mill owners, who is a mere tallow candle in this constellation, paid $7,000,000 for the title his daughter is now wearing. And this $7,000,000 must have been a mere bagatelle compared to what it cost Huntington to get the lively Hatzfeldt. The poor flour mill man could not have paid that fellow's "debts of honor." This buying of titles, however, is but one way by which the millionaires are beggaring the American people. So much of their time is now spent over there that they have come to look upon the United States as their rented farm, and Europe as the place where they, in their high roller way, must get rid of its income. Call to mind the millionaire families who live a large part of their time in Europe. Call to mind those who have made Europe their permanent home, with their income drawn from the United States. Call to mind the great European estates, that have been first cleared of their peasantry, and then leased by American millionaires, that they may have the exclusive right to shoot at something. Call to mind the New York City millionaire, who purchased an English estate, one to fit the title he is lick-spittling after, and where he can rest, after airing his mind in his great London Daily and Monthly; all three, estate and periodicals, being a source of loss, that is made good by American earned money. Call all these things to mind, and if we are poor in capital have we not found the reason why?

Europe is the Broadway of these people, and they are there to squander money, not to make it. And the European visitor to our shores does not make up the loss. He comes, looks at some of our landscape, Niagara, the Yosemite, etc., and is out of the country and home again. His is but a drop to the ocean we lose.

Need we wonder at our gold disappearing? Our bonds and stocks, Government and corporation, are scattered broadcast over the whole of Europe, and those decrepit titles, that were dying out, have been put on their feet again by American money, and are now living off the interest of American bonds of one kind or another.

Nor should we have to borrow foreign capital. It is over a century since this government was established, and it is time we had enough capital of our own.

But the United States Treasury is, and has been for over thirty years, the clearing house for the foreign holders of American securities. We are a mortgaged nation, and the office of our National Treasury is the place of all others where our foreign owners should get their interest. We are still in possession of the office, however, and in this we are ahead of Egypt, but it will take much hair-splitting to show any substantial difference in the results.

History does not contain, the imagination cannot evolve, a more damnable exhibition of incompetence than this failure of our scrub statesmen to extricate their country from the clutch of its foreign masters.

Ruling one or the three principal gold producers of the world, they are compelled to resort, to all the shifts known to the desperate bankrupt in order to keep a few millions of it in the Treasury, and thereby save our whole monetary system from going to the dogs. For let us not delude ourselves; the moment the United States

Treasury cannot give gold for its greenbacks, that moment will the history of the greenback begin to repeat itself. And we are not saving ourselves by making greenbacks lean on silver. They cannot be made stronger than the thing they lean on. Gold we must have as our standard.

We are in commercial relations with all nations, and the laws of trade are inexorable, and say: You must have money that is acceptable to those you buy from. Bring any other, and you can call the fifty cents it contains one hundred, but your laws are for the United States only, and you must accept the fifty cents or take back the mongrel that in your own barnyard crows so loud, for the United States has induced a swindle that she is powerless to enforce beyond her own borders.

No law is necessary to make us take gold. Just out of the mine or just out of the mint, we want it - the whole world wants it.

Finance, if not as old as the hills, is at least pretty near as old as the graves at the foot of them. There is nothing new to be learned regarding her laws. And those laws do not shut out tin, copper, paper, rags, nails, or silver from being used as money as long as it is agreeable to the interested. But the wisdom of the world comes from her experience, and if she calls for gold money it is because she has never found a better. All other kinds fade before it as fades the moon before the rising sun.

There is but one central orb in the world's monetary systems, and that is Gold. And its satellites, paper or silver, will never be able to get out of their orbits where the fixed and unalterable laws of the world's financial systems have placed them. Temporary disturbances may deceive the searcher, but he has mistaken his calling who cannot distinguish planets from the sun around which they are moving.

The different governments of Europe, that are not gold producers, have gold as the basis of their monetary systems, and, what is more, the gold is there. The United States, that is a gold producer, would also have it as the basis of its monetary system, but this nation, the one independent nation that is all extensive and the leading producer of the metal that the enlightened world approves of as making the best of all moneys, cannot retain enough of it to give future stability to her own currency.

This nation, the greatest of to-day, or any day!

This nation, that has given more to the rest of the world than it has ever received!

This nation - of all others on this earth - must be content with the money of the enslaved East Indian coolie; must be content with the money of the decaying Chinaman; must be content with the money of the half savage republics to the south of us!

This nation, whose chief magistrate is the embodiment of power never dreamed of by the Caesars and Napoleons in their palmiest days! This nation, that is impregnable against the combined armies of the world, is being sapped and mined of its wealth under the very eyes of its driveling lawmakers, and silver is becoming the badge of its humiliation and inferiority!

XIV.

The national debt of France is $7,000,000,000. This exceeds the combined national debts of the United States, England, and Germany.

In territory, France is not as large as California.

Her population is[2] 37,000,000
The population of the United States is 65,000,000
The population of England is 37,000,000
The population of Germany is 40,000,000

———————

Total 142,000,000

The French navy is a fairly close second to that of England.

Her army is as large as that of Germany.

France, then, supports an army and navy of the first class, and has only 37,000,000 people to do it with. And this same 37,000,000 people pays interest on a debt that is greater than that of the 142,000,000 people in the three countries named. Yet there is no wail of distress, such as we are familiar with, heard in this France, with its great army and navy, and its fabulous interest-bearing, debt.

What is the secret of it?

France is the greatest producer of luxeries in the world, and, of course, has the rich the world over for her customers; and she is a nation of small owners, her resources, land and all else, being subdivided among her people to an extent unknown elsewhere. This is only half the secret.

There is a natural increase of wealth in every country. Keep that natural increase in the country where it is made, and there will always be a surplus left after the mere live and wear expenses are paid, and this surplus can be used either to support an army or to build macadamized roads. This then is the other half, without which she would be where we are: France legislates to keep her wealth in her own country - and her loss on that canal is only one plum out of her heeping bushel.

The foreign sapper and miner does no work on French soil. His field of operation is the whole American continent, beginning in Canada and on down through, without a skip, till he reaches Magellan and the Horn, scattering his due bills all the way.

The French law-maker, in spite of his clatter, is without a peer, and he dwarfs none so much as our own, who will become the butt of his own sneer if he ever gets his eyes open.

This foreign master of the art of governing legislates in the interests of his own people, who are the only source of his country's power or greatness, and he leaves the income of the large farm or small one where it is made. And when the issuing of bonds is the only alternative he issues them in sizes those small incomes can buy.

Their labor pays the debt in the end, and it is their interests that are first consulted when profits from bond issues are considered. He makes the size of the bond fit their ability to buy, and not that of the millionaire syndicate, as is the case in this misgoverned land, where the matchless ignorance and complicity of the law-maker is made to serve the matchless corruption and greed of its millionaire master.

No French syndicate makes its five to ten per cent. profits off every issue of bonds.

Thousands among our toilers could have secured their ten-dollar savings could they have bought Government bonds of that denomination but they could not, and were forced to become the victims of swindling bankers.

Individual greed cares nothing for its victims as they are thrown on the streets and its ways.

When this enterprising foreigner, with his surplus capital, the result of wise laws, started for Panama to do a much needed work for this Western world, that this great gold producing country could not find the capital to do, our blackmailers worked the Monroe Doctrine on him and all the while he was quieting the rascals, the sappers and miners were splitting their sides at our treasury door.

Congress is opened by a chaplain. It should be opened by a physician and a warrant - bibs for the drooling chins of some and the rest to jail.

[2] The writer is not within hundreds of miles of works of reference; but these figures are substantially correct. The quibbler, however, is welcome to anything he may find.

Conclusion.

A policy that keeps our increase of wealth in the country, and prevents it from lodging in a few hands, can work no injury whatever. No enterprise worthy of notice will languish for the want of the necessary capital. The savings banks are the depositories of the people, and the capital of those institution in all the cities of the country exceeds that of the commercial or capitalistic banks, and the "statements" of the savings banks should dispel any fears as to whether capital can be concentrated afterit once gets into the hands of the people. $50,000,000 is the assets of more than one savings bank in the City of New York. And our own San Francisco has its Hibernia and other banks of its kind, with from $5,000,000 to $30,000,000 of capital. And when it is remembered that the total deposits of an individual in most of those institutions is not allowed to exceed $3,000, we can see that the people will not fail us as "concentrators" when their help is needed.

Those statements also show whether those of small means are for concealing it, or for putting it into the hands of competent managers for investment. And if these competent managers approve of an enterprise they will not neglect their client's interests by refusing to make the required loan.

At present, they do not seek investment outside of corporate limits, and, of course, the money they have been intrusted with, must be about all invested, and cannot be called idle money, or there could be no interest paid to its owners.

There will be no friction in the management of industrial enterprises when this savings-bank depositor makes a direct investment. The voter at the polls has his say as to who shall fill a political office, but he cannot interfere in the work of the office itself. Neither will our investor have the right or power to interfere. In short, the modern industrial world would go to pieces even now, if it was run by its million owners, instead of by its appointed or elected superintendent.

These small depositors are either laborers or in "business;" business that they would enlarge if business of all kinds was not already overdone. It is not to be inferred from this that the new law will cause factories to run day and night, or keep the merchant's door always on the swing. There will be an increase of business surely; but this world is not like a goose whose liver we are after. Her capacity to absorb what we make or produce is limited, and when we reach that limit, let us be content, and chain down Greed for the moment, that we may look out and see how beautiful is this world whereon we live, when freed from the crack of the master's whip.

-

Through Confiscation alone can the people regain their liberty and possession of their resources.

A readjustment means justice to all.

Without it the days of the republic are numbered, and the overwhelming disaster to mankind will mark the burial place of the aspirations of its founders, and the latest conquest of individual greed.

That disaster cannot be averted by Grover Cleveland, the head of the Democratic party, finding a foreign market for a few more ship-loads of our products. And never should the oppressed of other lands find an enemy here to take their bread. Pinching nature has not made wolves of this people that they should go and show their teeth among the cabins and hovels of Europe. Theirs is but a crust now, and a judgement should wither the hand that would take it from them.

This disaster cannot be averted by Thomas B. Reed, the idol and recognized leader of the Republican party, forcing the producers of those few ship loads of products to consume them themselves. The whole could be dropped to the bottom of the sea, or sold for their value a hundred fold, and it would not stay the doom of the Republic one swing of the pendulum.

This disaster cannot be averted by Robert G. Ingersoll - another idol - advising the millionaire to be extravagant. Or by taking the labor-saving machinery away from the people, and keeping them longer at their toil, as this humbug has suggested.

This Is The Age Of Beef.

Our leaders are incompetent. Argument here is needless. We have plenty of everything, and plenty of hunger at the same time, which shows mismanagement. Our leaders, therefore, must be incompetent. Nor should the blame of this be charged to the people. Statecraft, like the prescribing of medicine or the practice of law, is a profession, and the unlearned in their ways is at the mercy of the quacks of all three.

When none but quacks offer their services to the State a selection must be made, and the people cannot be held to account for choosing quacks when there was nothing to choose from but quacks.

Whatever physical characteristics distinguishes the genius of leadership from the ordinary man; whether it is long legs or short; long nose or pug; big heads or little, one thing is certain - history tells you on her every page that leadership is never found in combination with beef. Cleveland and Reed! How they stew and swelter in positions they cannot fill. How these Jonahs have grown till they have become the whale itself. How their fat will spot the pages to come, and float on the sea where the Republic went down.

And Ingersoll - let us not forget Ingersoll - the thumber over of past woes, whose five hundred dollar opera ticket identifies the class to which he now belongs, and proves his success as a fifteenth century reformer. The people made and keep up the acquaintance of this man by way of the ticket office, but instead of considering him as they would any other footlight performer, who had struck a paying vein and was working it for all it was worth, and who can only be heard at so much per ticket, they have come to look upon the character he has been acting as the man himself, and their friend who would make their cause his own.

No fee is collected at the door of the little church that is found along the byways of every Christian land, and its humble preacher can be heard free of cost. But abuse of this follower and disciple of Jesus, whose teachings are in no way responsible for the crimes of Individual Greed, has been the source of large profits to this man, who has even gone so far as to tell his hearers not to give a dollar to the support of a preacher - meaning, doubtless, while you could see his performance for half the money.

This man, whose audience is world-wide, uses his great opportunity for helping mankind by inclosing the scenes of former struggles, and collecting the gate receipts.

This bogus friend of the people answers the cry of distress that is heard all over this bountiful land by a shrug, and a nod to the master to drop a few more crumbs, as if the people were hungry dogs under the table.

Ingersoll a friend of the oppressed? He would render justice to the enslaved toiler by lengthening his hours of labor.

A sham reformer, who would destroy the Inquisition of this day by plunging his spotless blade into an Inquisition whose sun has set, never to rise again.

Ingersoll of the tender soul, who shows the sincerity of his exhibition-tears for the persecuted dead by riding, rough-shod, over the sensibilities of the blameless living.

Warrior Ingersoll, furiously charging up and down an abandoned battle-field, rattling the bleaching bones of a dead and gone enemy - for an admission fee.

Ingersoll the capper, who would turn all eyes to the ashes of a burned-out bell, while another is being dug in our rear.

Cleveland - Reed - Ingersoll,

The Three

C A G L I O S T R O S.